"Crafting Your Perfect Picnic Table"

This book explores the creation of a specific and highly popular style of picnic table, focusing on both design and size. It includes two detailed project plans, both featuring the same design but using different lumber sizes. You'll have the flexibility to choose between two common lumber sizes: 2x6 (50x150 mm) or 2x4 (50x100 mm).

The designs showcase sturdy, solid picnic tables with wider tabletops compared to most standard designs.

Build Your Own Six-Seater Picnic Table

Building with 2x4 (50x100 mm)
and 2x6 (50x150 mm) Lumber

Vol. 1

By Les Kenny

Les Kenny, 1948-

Build Your Own Six-Seater Picnic Table

Building with 2x4 (50x100 mm) and 2x6 (50x150 mm) Lumber, Vol. 1

Copyright © Les Kenny 2024

ISBN 978-1-7635730-2-4

leskenny.com

Table of Contents

Project 1. Using 2x4 (50x100mm) lumber

Table of Contents

Project 2. Using 2x6 (50x150mm) lumber

Build Your Own
Six-Seater Picnic Table

Using 2 x 4 (50 x 100 mm) lumber

Step-by-step guide

Description

This picnic table is constructed out of 2 x 4 (50 x 100 mm) lumber. It will comfortably seat 6 people. Wide seats positioned both in terms of height and distance from the tabletop ensures easy access and maximum comfort.

Dimensions:
- Length: 6' 6¾" (2 m).
- Width: 67" (1700 mm).
- Height: 29⅞" (758 mm).
- Tabletop width: 34¼" (870 mm).

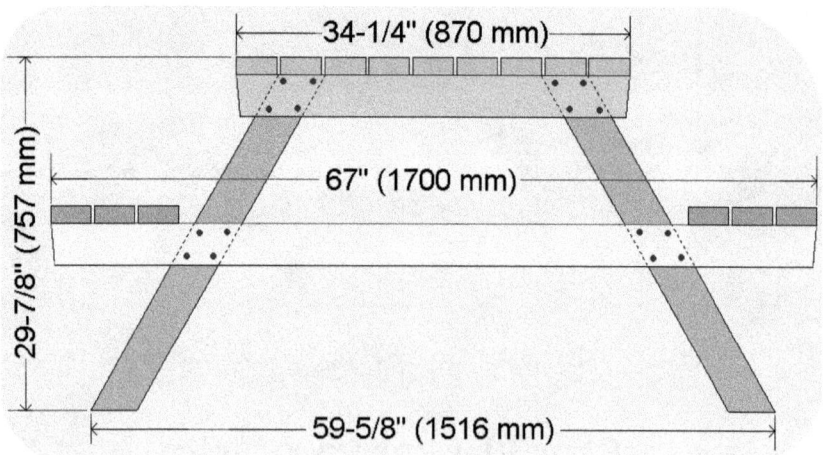

2

Part identification

[a] Leg	**[e]** Seat board
[b] Middle rail	**[f]** Seat cleat
[c] Top rail	**[g]** Table cleat
[d] Tabletop board	**[h]** Brace

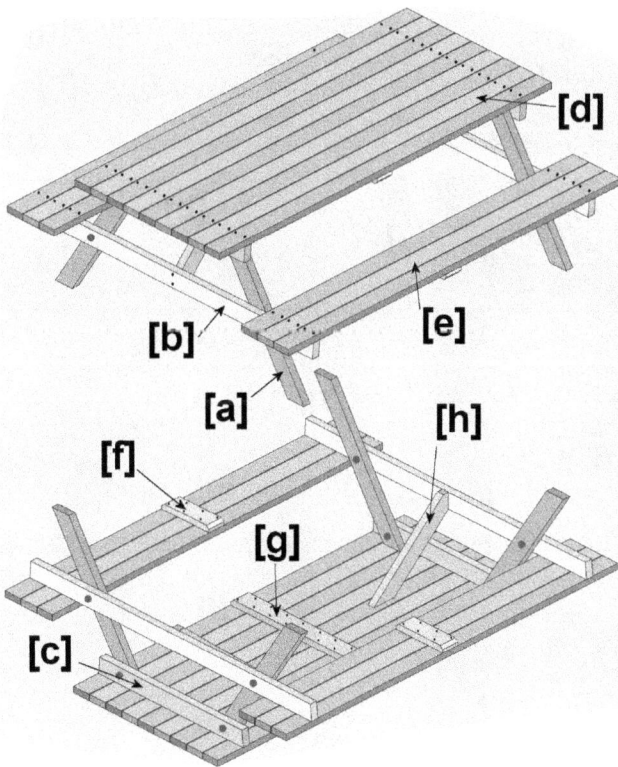

Plans:
Imperial measurements

Below are the picnic table plans, with dimensions given in inches and fractions of an inch.

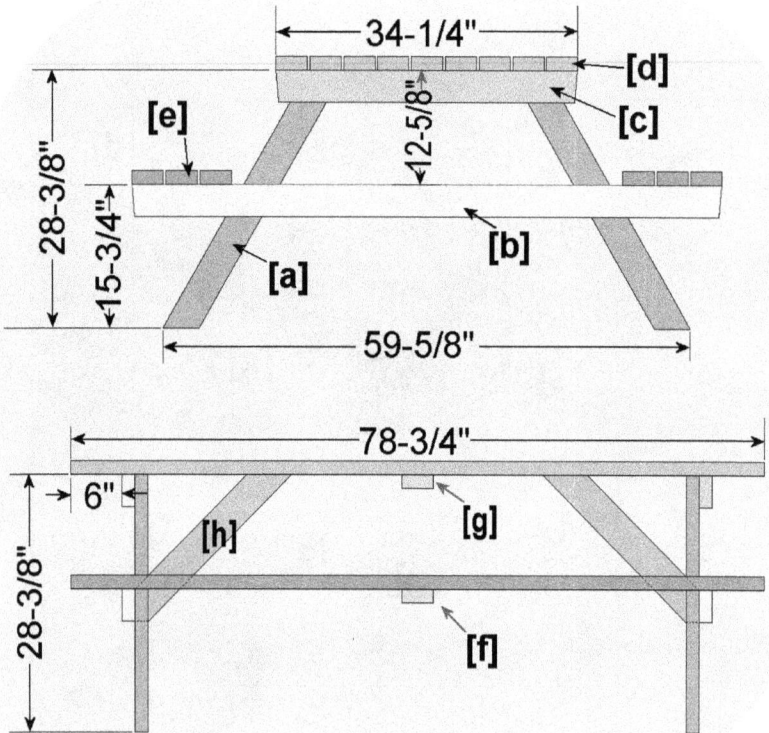

Plans:
Metric measurements

Below are the picnic table plans, with dimensions given in millimeters.

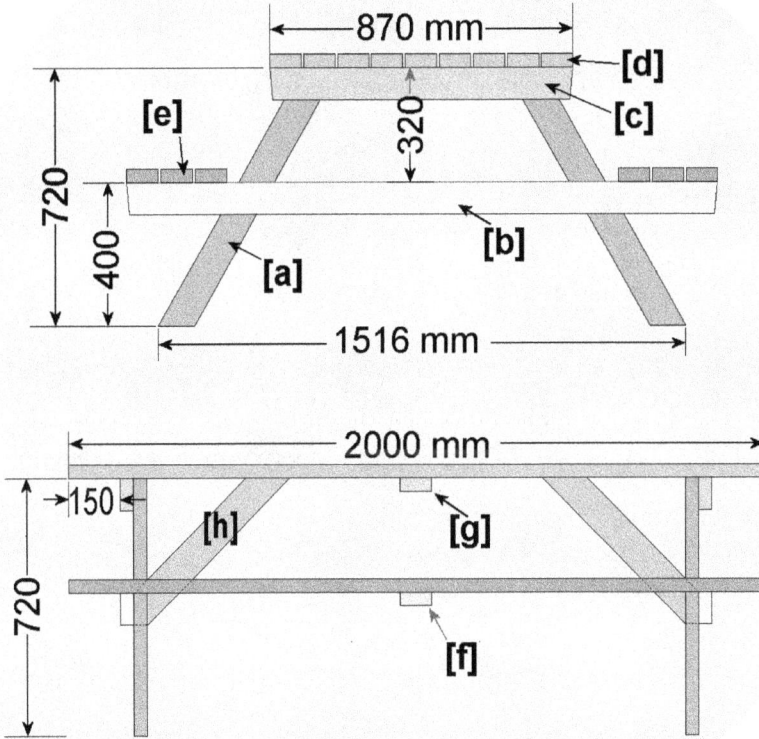

About the measurements

Length measurements in this project are provided in both imperial units (inches) and metric units (millimeters).

When measurements are presented side by side, the inch measurements are listed first, followed by the metric equivalents in parentheses.

For example: 15-3/4" (400 mm).

The example above refers to the length of a piece of wood. Below is an example showing the size (width and thickness) of pieces of wood:

2 x 4 (50 x 100 mm) means that the wood is 2 inches thick and 4 inches wide, or, in metric terms, 50 millimeters thick and 100 millimeters wide.

Shopping list: Lumber

Wood size	Length	Qty
2 x 4 (50 x 100 mm)	8 ft (2.4 m)	10
2 x 4 (50 x 100 mm)	10 ft (3 m)	7

The lengths provided above are standard stock sizes, which means they are commonly found at major lumber retailers and home improvement centers.

From these listed lengths, you will be able to cut all the pieces required for the construction of the picnic table.

The **cutting plan** shows how to cut all the pieces from the specified lengths to minimize waste.

When purchasing wood for the picnic table, it is advisable to buy dressed lumber, which is wood that has been planed (made smooth).

Shopping list: Fixings

Exterior wood screws:

- 72 screws 3" (75 mm) long.
- 60 screws 3½" (90 mm) long.

1/2" (12 mm) galvanized coach/carriage bolts:

- 8 bolts 4" (100 mm) long.
- 8 each nuts and washers to match.

Note: Use the 3" (75 mm) screws for the frames, cleats, and braces.
Use the 3½" (90 mm) screws for the seat boards and the tabletop boards.

Dressed lumber

Dressed lumber is wood that has been planed and smoothed, which makes it smaller than the nominal sizes given.

For example, 2 x 4 (50 x 100 mm) dressed lumber will be 1½" x 3½" (38 x 89 mm) in actual size.

Different countries and regions may have size variations.

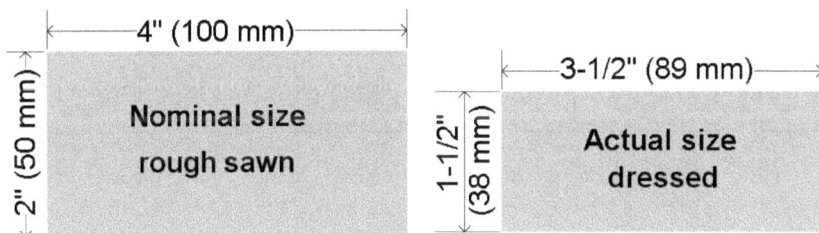

The difference in size will not impact the build as it is the lengths of the pieces that are important, not so much the width and thickness of the wood.

Cutting list

2 x 4 (50 x 100 mm) lumber		
Piece ID	**Length**	**Qty**
[a]	34¾" (883 mm)	4
[b]	67" (1700 mm)	2
[c]	34¼" (870 mm)	2
[d]	78¾" (2000 mm)	9
[e]	78¾" (2000 mm)	6
[f]	11¼" (285 mm)	2
[g]	34¼" (870 mm)	1
[h]	25" (635 mm)	2

INSTRUCTIONS

Start the build

Let's go!

Step 1. Cut all the pieces

Out of 2 x 4 (50 x 100 mm) lumber, cut all the pieces to the lengths given in the **'Cutting list'**, and also below the drawing.

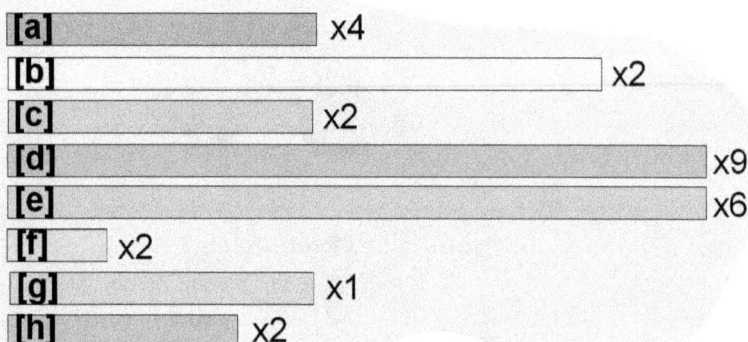

[a] x4
[b] x2
[c] x2
[d] x9
[e] x6
[f] x2
[g] x1
[h] x2

[a] 34-3/4" (883 mm) long, cut 4 pieces

[b] 67" (1700 mm) long, cut 2 pieces

[c] 34-1/4" (870 mm) long, cut 2 pieces

[d] 78-3/4" (2000 mm) long, cut 9 pieces

[e] 78-3/4" (2000 mm) long, cut 6 pieces

[f] 11-1/4" (285 mm) long, cut 2 pieces

[g] 34-1/4" (870 mm) long, cut 1 piece

[h] 25" (635 mm) long, cut 2 pieces

Cutting plan

All the pieces can be cut from the standard stock lengths that are listed in the '**Shopping list**'.

The drawing below demonstrates how to cut all the components from the following pieces of 2 x 4 (50 x 100 mm) lumber.

• 10 pieces that are 8 ft (2.4 m) long.
• 7 pieces that are 10 ft (3 m) long.

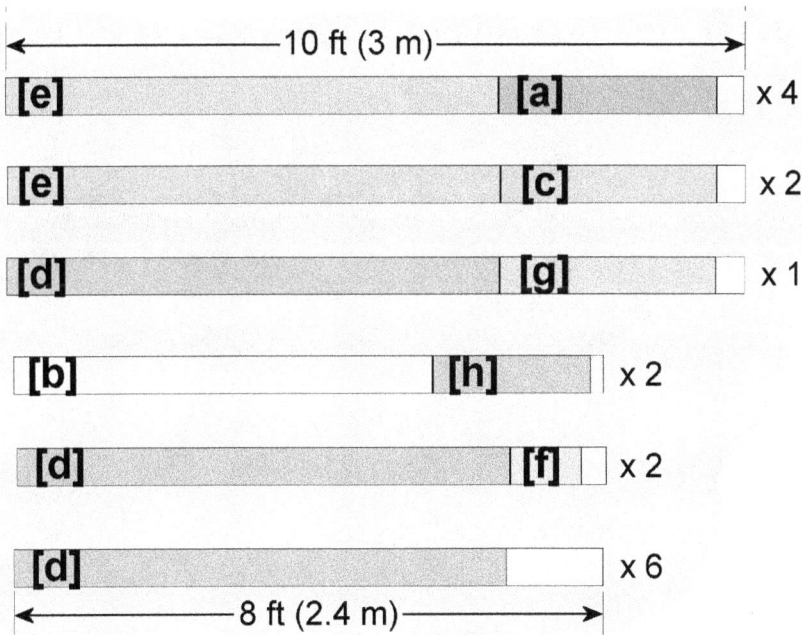

|←————— 10 ft (3 m) —————→|

| [e] | [a] | x 4 |

| [e] | [c] | x 2 |

| [d] | [g] | x 1 |

| [b] | [h] | x 2 |

| [d] | [f] | x 2 |

| [d] | | x 6 |

|←————— 8 ft (2.4 m) —————→|

Step 2. Cut the angles

Once all the pieces are cut to length, pieces [a], [b], [c], and [h] need to have the ends cut at an angle. Cut the angles according to the list and illustration below.

[a] For the legs, cut a 30° angle each end.
[b] For the middle rail, cut a 5° angle each end.
[c] For the top rail, cut a 5° angle each end.
[h] For the braces, cut a 45° angle each end.

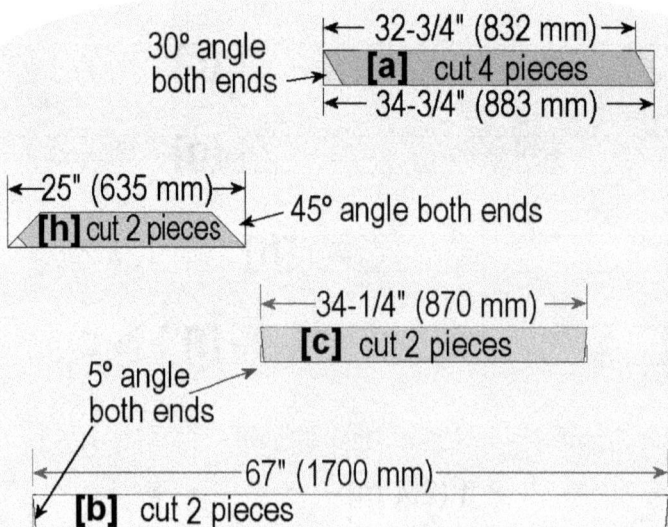

30° angle both ends →
← 32-3/4" (832 mm) →
[a] cut 4 pieces
← 34-3/4" (883 mm) →

←25" (635 mm)→
[h] cut 2 pieces
45° angle both ends

←34-1/4" (870 mm) →
[c] cut 2 pieces

5° angle both ends
←67" (1700 mm)→
[b] cut 2 pieces

Ready to assemble

At this stage, you should have all the pieces cut as shown below, ready for assembly.

[a] Leg — 4 pieces

[b] Middle rail — 2 pieces

[c] Top rail — 2 pieces

[d] Tabletop board — 9 pieces

[e] Seat board — 6 pieces

[f] Seat cleat — 2 pieces

[g] Table cleat — 1 piece

[h] Brace — 2 pieces

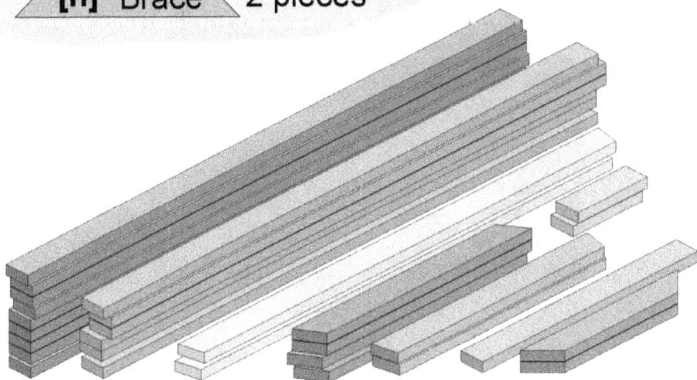

Step 3. Arrange the legs

Lay each pair of legs flat on an even surface, spaced according to the plan drawing below. Use a straight-edge to ensure the bottom of both legs are in-line.

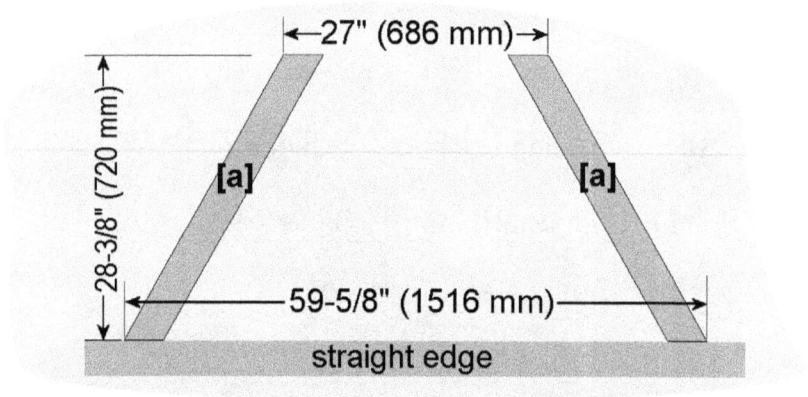

27" (686 mm)

28-3/8" (720 mm)

[a]   [a]

59-5/8" (1516 mm)

straight edge

Straight edge to align the legs to

Step 4. Assemble the frames

Place cross rails **[b]** and **[c]** on legs **[a]** according to the plan drawing below.
Use four 3" (75 mm) screws at each joint, as illustrated in the drawing. Do not place screws in the middle of a joint, as that space is reserved for a bolt.

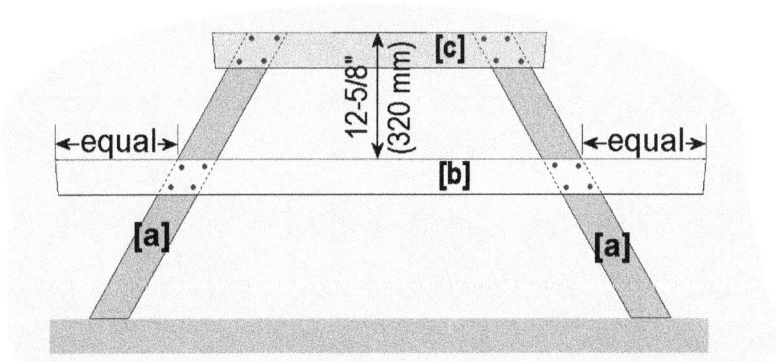

Screwing

Whenever you're fastening two pieces of wood together with screws, it's important to predrill a **clearance hole** through the top piece.

A **clearance hole** should have the same diameter or slightly larger (but never smaller) than the outside diameter of the screw threads.

This allows the screw to go through the top piece smoothly, with the threads only gripping into the bottom piece, ensuring a tight connection between the two parts.

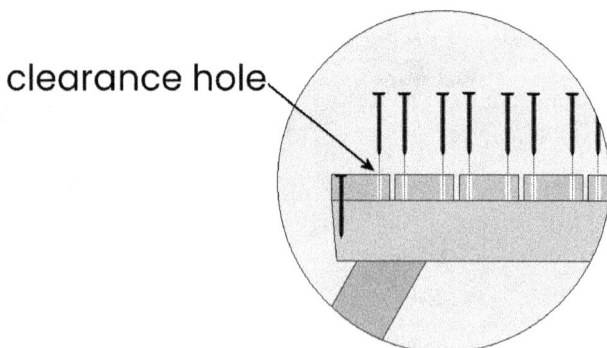

clearance hole

Step 5. Stand the frames

Clamp a block flush to the bottom of each leg, as illustrated in the drawing below. This allows the frames to stand by themselves. Hence, you can position the frames and place the boards without needing help from another person to hold the frames upright.

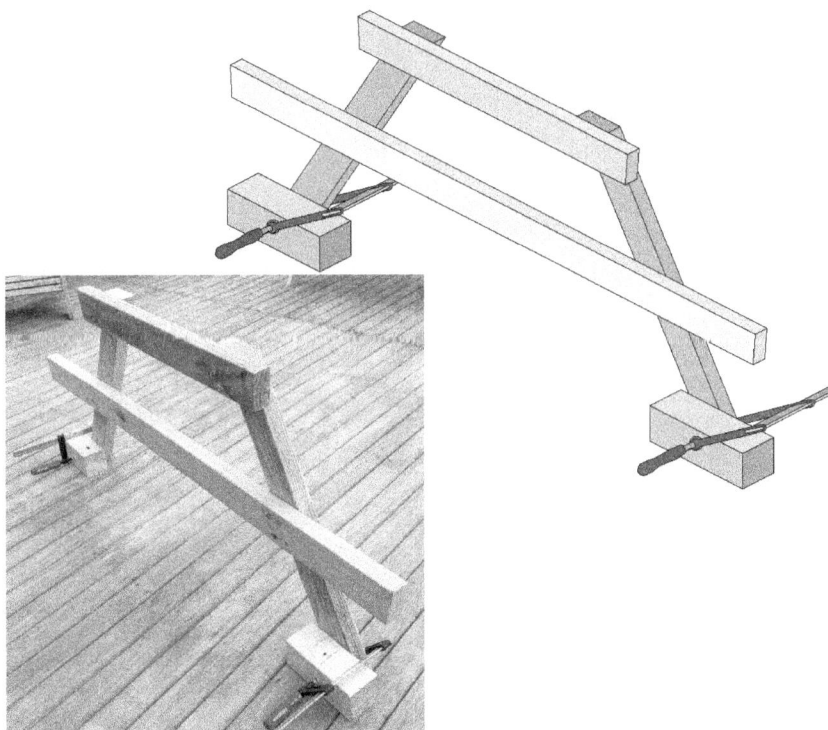

Step 6. Space the frames

Now, space the frames approximately so that when the tabletop and seat boards are positioned, they will overhang the frames at each end by 6" (150 mm).

Step 7. Put on the outer boards

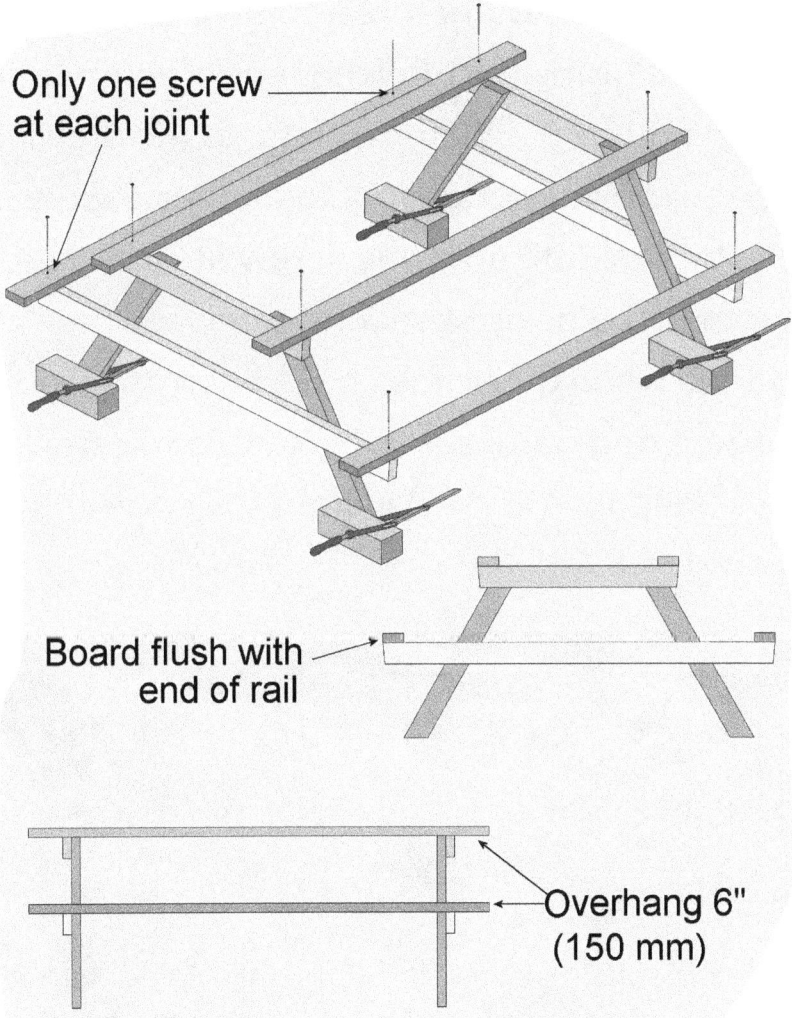

Only one screw at each joint

Board flush with end of rail

Overhang 6"
(150 mm)

Put on the outer boards [explanation]

First, place the outer tabletop and seat boards onto the frame rails, having them overhang each end by 6" (150 mm). Refer to the drawing on the previous page for placement. Secure the boards with **only one screw** at each joint – for the time being. A second screw will be added when the frames have been checked square and parallel. Use 3½" (90 mm) screws positioned ⅝" (15 mm) in from the edge of the board.

Is it square and parallel?

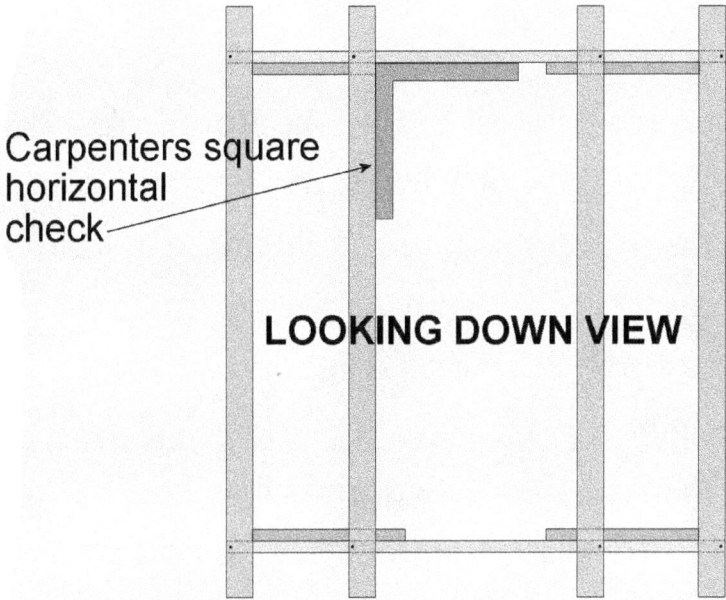

Carpenters square horizontal check

LOOKING DOWN VIEW

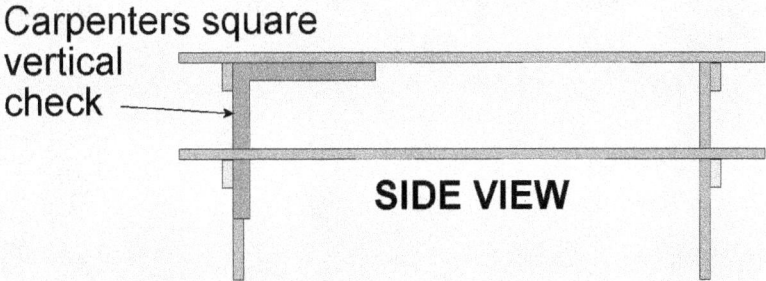

Carpenters square vertical check

SIDE VIEW

Is it square and parallel? [explanation]

Check that the frames are parallel, and with a carpenter's square ensure the frames are square (at right angles) to the tabletop and seat boards, both horizontally and vertically. If necessary, make any straightening adjustments, then add a second screw to each joint.
This will hold the unit square while you continue to add the intermediate boards.

Step 8. Add the intermediate boards

Place the intermediate boards. Ensure the ends are flush and the gaps between the boards are even. Draw a 'screw line ' across the table and seats to keep the screws in a straight line.

Step 9. Attach the cleats

With the table upside-down, screw cleats across the center of the seats and the tabletop. Use two 3" (75 mm) screws positioned diagonally across each joint.

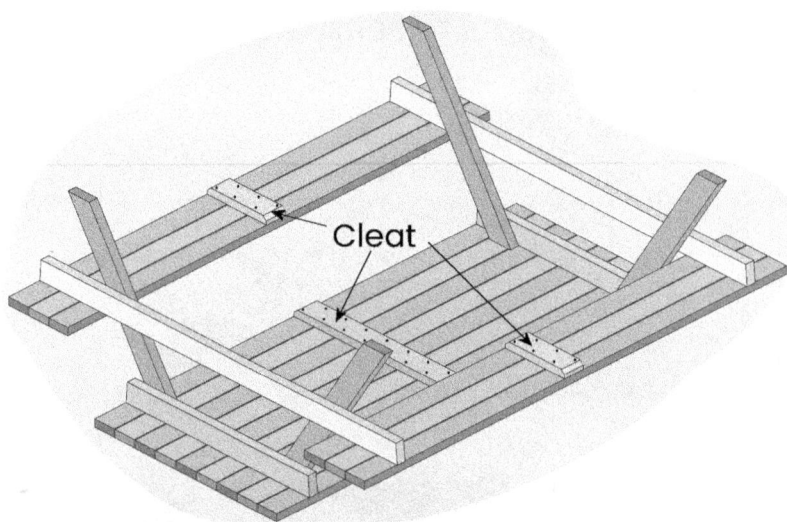

Cleat

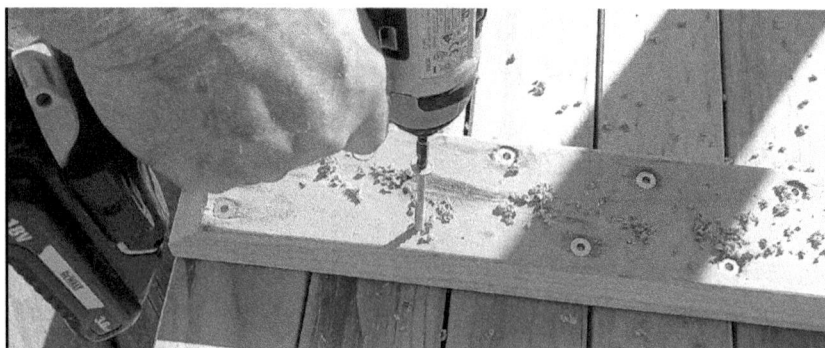

Step 10. Add the bracing

Ensure the end-frames are square (upright) to the tabletop, and then position each brace as shown in the image below. Screw one end of the brace to the middle rail with two 3" (75 mm) screws, and the other end with 3 screws angled into the tabletop.

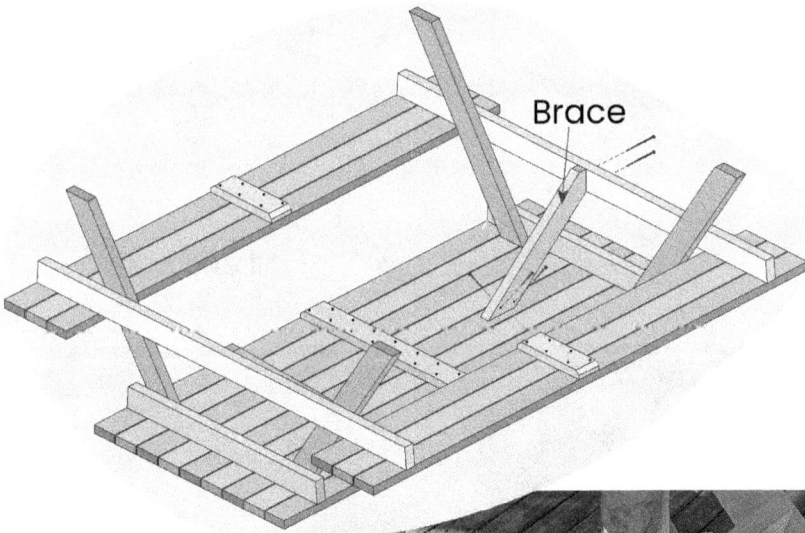

Brace

Step 11. Drill and bolt

Drill a bolt hole through the center of every leg and rail joint - eight altogether.
Insert 1/2" (12 mm) galvanised bolts, add washers and nuts, and tighten them up.

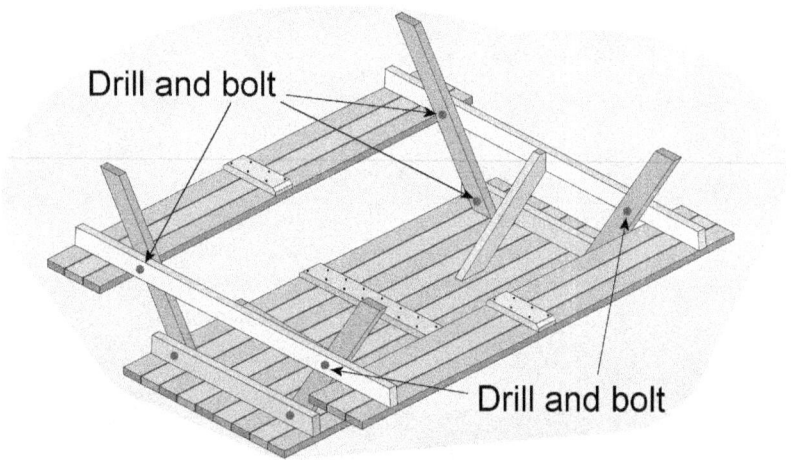

Drill and bolt

Drill and bolt

All finished!

And there it is.

A nice solid, comfortable picnic table that will seat at least six people.

Project #2

Build Your Own
Six-Seater Picnic Table

Using 2 x 6 (50 x 150 mm) lumber

Step-by-step guide

Description

This picnic table is constructed out of 2 x 6 (50 x 150 mm) lumber. It will comfortably seat 6 people. Wide seats positioned both in terms of height and distance from the tabletop ensures easy access and maximum comfort.

Dimensions:
- Length: 6' 6¾" (2 meters).
- Width: 67" (1700 mm).
- Height: 29⅞" (758 mm).
- Tabletop width: 34¼" (870 mm).

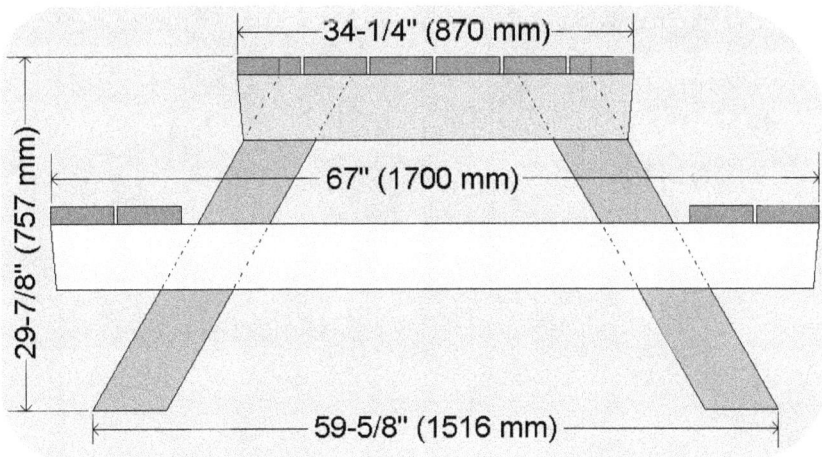

Part identification

[a] Leg	**[e]** Seat board
[b] Middle rail	**[f]** Seat cleat
[c] Top rail	**[g]** Table cleat
[d] Tabletop board	**[h]** Brace

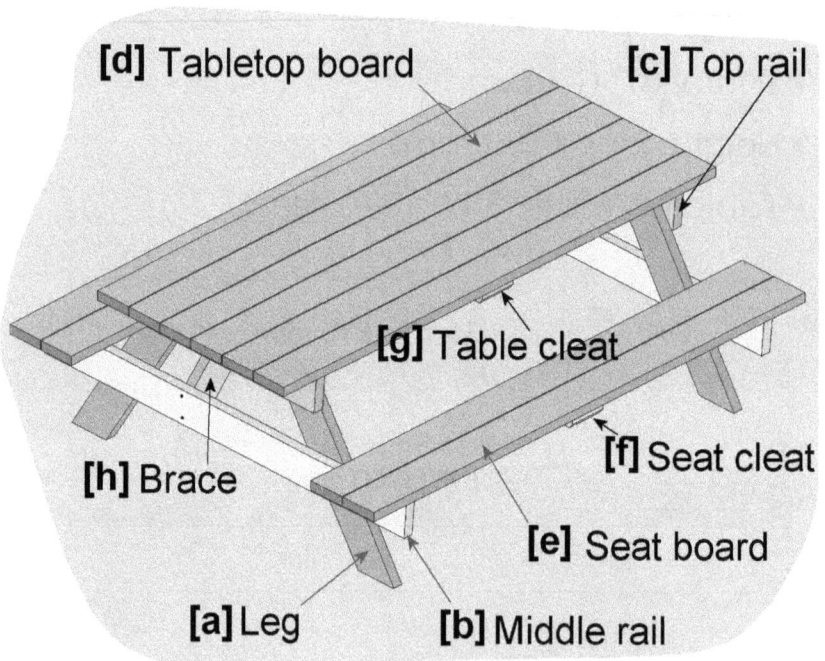

[d] Tabletop board

[c] Top rail

[g] Table cleat

[f] Seat cleat

[h] Brace

[e] Seat board

[a] Leg

[b] Middle rail

Plans - Imperial units

Below are the picnic table plans, with dimensions given in inches and fractions of an inch.

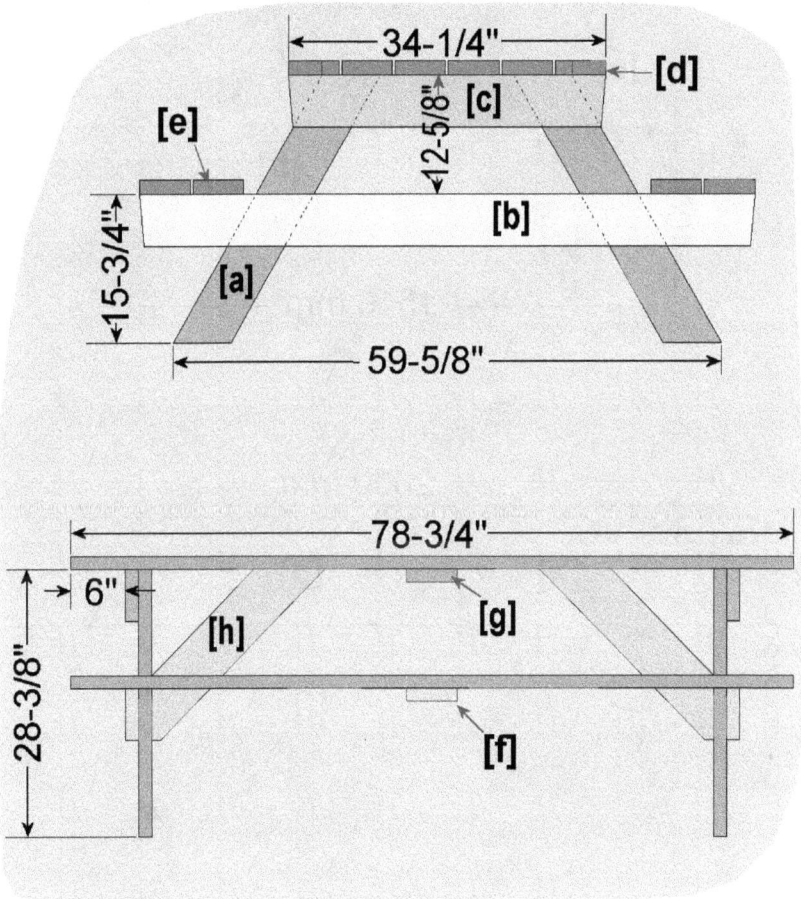

Plans - Metric units

Below are the picnic table plans, with dimensions given in millimeters.

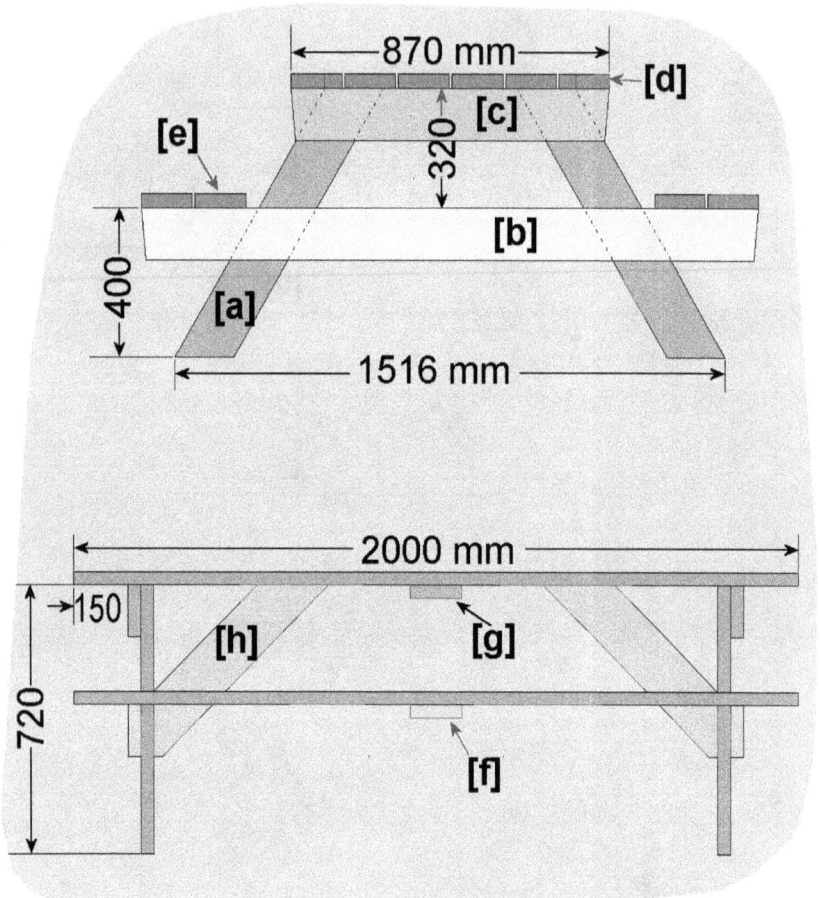

About the measurements

Length measurements in this project are given in both imperial units (inches) and metric units (millimeters).

When the measurements are presented side by side, the inch measurements are given first followed by the metric equivalent in brackets.

For example: 15-3/4" (400 mm).

The example above refers to the length of a piece of wood. Below is an example showing the size (width and thickness) of pieces of wood:

2 x 6 (50 x 150 mm) means that the wood is 2 inches thick and 6 inches wide, or, in metric terms, 50 millimeters thick and 150 millimeters wide.

Shopping list: Lumber

Wood size	Length	Qty
2 x 6 (50 x 150 mm)	8 ft (2.4 m)	2
2 x 6 (50 x 150 mm)	10 ft (3 m)	7
2 x 6 (50 x 150 mm)	12 ft (3.6 m)	2

The lengths provided above are standard stock sizes, which means they are commonly found at major lumber retailers and home improvement centers. When purchasing select a dressed lumber, which is wood that has been planed (made smooth).

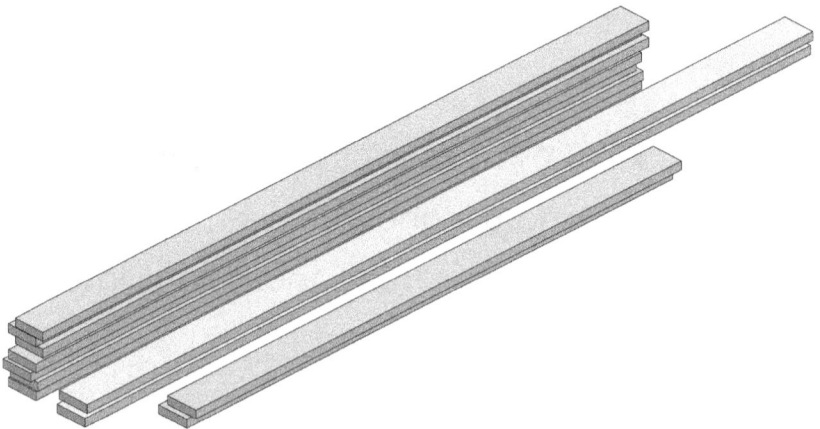

Shopping list: Fixings

Exterior wood screws:

- 62 screws 3" (75 mm) long.
- 40 screws 3½" (90 mm) long.

1/2" (12 mm) galvanized coach/carriage bolts:

- 8 bolts 4" (100 mm) long.
- 8 each nuts and washers to match.

Note: Use the 3" (75 mm) screws for the frames, cleats, and braces.
Use the 3½" (90 mm) screws for the seat boards and the tabletop boards.

Dressed lumber

Dressed lumber is wood that has been planed and smoothed, which makes it smaller than the nominal sizes given.

For example, 2 x 6 (50 x 150 mm) dressed lumber will be 1½" x 5½" (38 x 140 mm) in actual size.

Different countries and regions may have size variations.

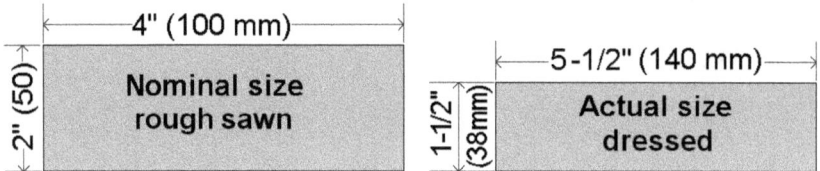

4" (100 mm)	**5-1/2" (140 mm)**
2" (50) Nominal size rough sawn	**1-1/2" (38mm)** Actual size dressed

The difference in size will not impact the build as it is the lengths of the pieces that are important, not so much the width and thickness of the wood.

Cutting list

2 x 6 (50 x 150 mm) lumber		
Piece ID	**Length**	**Qty**
[a]	36" (912 mm)	4
[b]	67" (1700 mm)	2
[c]	34¼" (870 mm)	2
[d]	78¾" (2000 mm)	6
[e]	78¾" (2000 mm)	4
[f]	11¼" (285 mm)	2
[g]	34¼" (870 mm)	1
[h]	28⅞" (734 mm)	2

INSTRUCTIONS

Start the build

Step 1. Cut all the pieces

Cut all the pieces to the lengths given in the **Cutting list**.

All the pieces can be cut from the standard stock lengths that are listed in the **Shopping list**.

Following on the next page is a **Cutting plan** showing how all the pieces can be cut from the standard lengths of lumber given in the **Shopping list**.

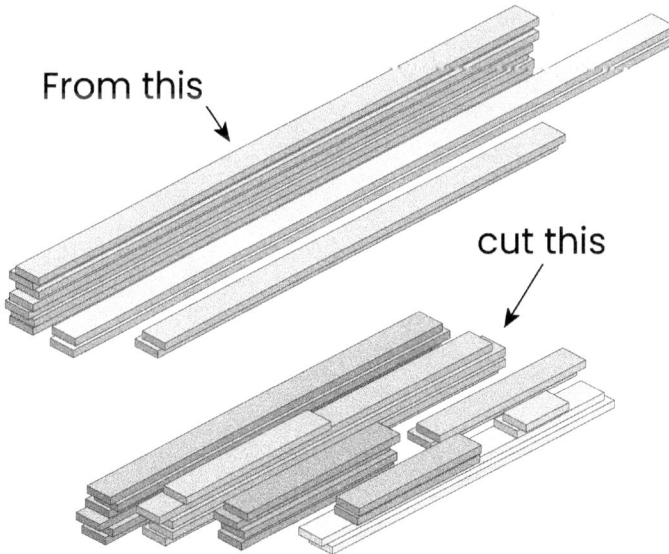

From this

cut this

Cutting plan

The drawing below shows how to cut all the required pieces from the stock lengths given in the **Shopping list**, which were...

- 2 pieces, 8 ft (2.4 m) long.
- 7 pieces, 10 ft (3 m) long.
- 2 pieces, 12 ft (3.6 m) long.

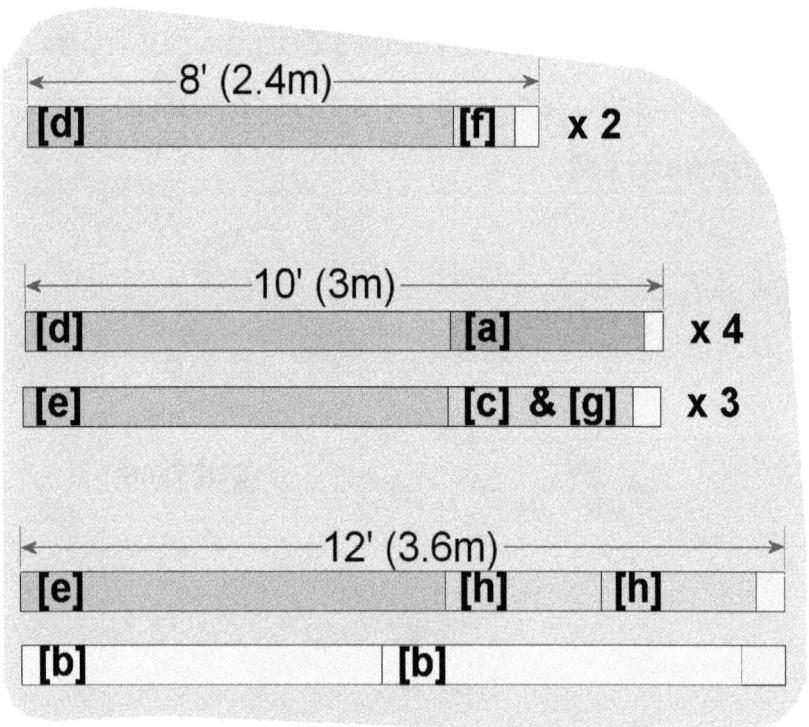

8' (2.4m)
[d]   [f]   x 2

10' (3m)
[d]   [a]   x 4
[e]   [c] & [g]   x 3

12' (3.6m)
[e]   [h]   [h]
[b]   [b]

Step 2. Cut the angles

Once all the pieces are cut to length, pieces **[a]**, **[b]**, **[c]**, and **[h]** need to have the ends cut at an angle.

Cut the angles according to the list and drawing below.

[a] For the legs, cut a 30° angle each end.

[b] For the middle rail, cut a 5° angle each end.

[c] For the top rail, cut a 5° angle each end.

[h] For the braces, cut a 45° angle each end.

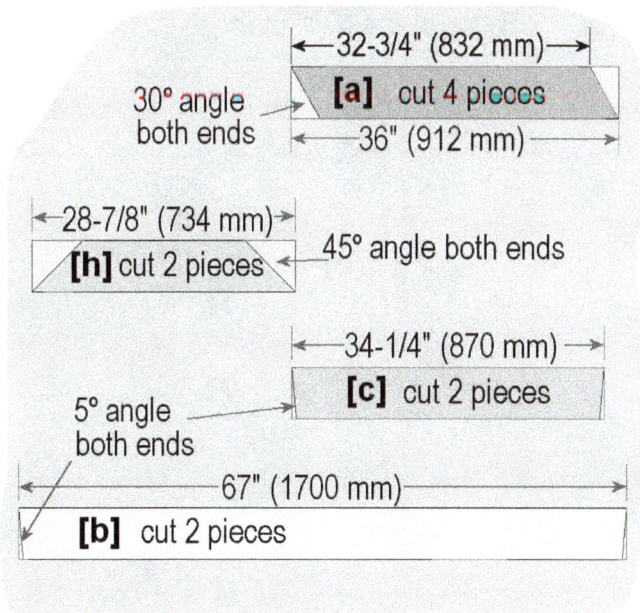

30° angle both ends

←—32-3/4" (832 mm)—→
[a] cut 4 pieces
←—36" (912 mm)—→

←28-7/8" (734 mm)→
[h] cut 2 pieces
45° angle both ends

←—34-1/4" (870 mm)—→
[c] cut 2 pieces

5° angle both ends

←—67" (1700 mm)—→
[b] cut 2 pieces

Ready to assemble

At this stage, you should have all the pieces cut as shown below, ready for assembly.

[a]	Leg	4 pieces
[b]	Middle rail	2 pieces
[c]	Top rail	2 pieces
[d]	Tabletop board	6 pieces
[e]	Seat board	4 pieces
[f]	Seat cleat	2 pieces
[g]	Table cleat	1 piece
[h]	Brace	2 pieces

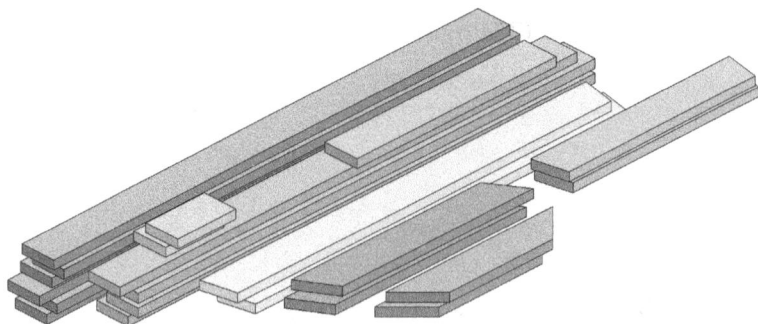

Step 3. Arrange the legs

Lay each pair of legs flat on an even surface, spacing them according to the plan drawing below. Use a straightedge to ensure the bottom of both legs are in-line.

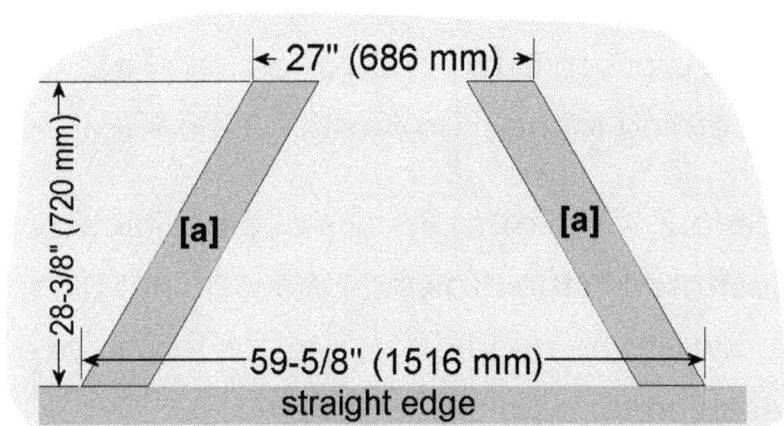

27" (686 mm)

28-3/8" (720 mm)

[a] [a]

59-5/8" (1516 mm)

straight edge

Straight edge to align the legs to

Step 4. Assemble the frames

Note: Have the frames assembled with them lying flat on even ground or on top of a suitable work bench.

Place cross rails **[b]** and **[c]** on legs **[a]** according to the plan drawing below.

Use four 3" (75 mm) screws at each joint, as illustrated in the drawing below. Do not place screws in the middle of a joint, as that space is reserved for a bolt.

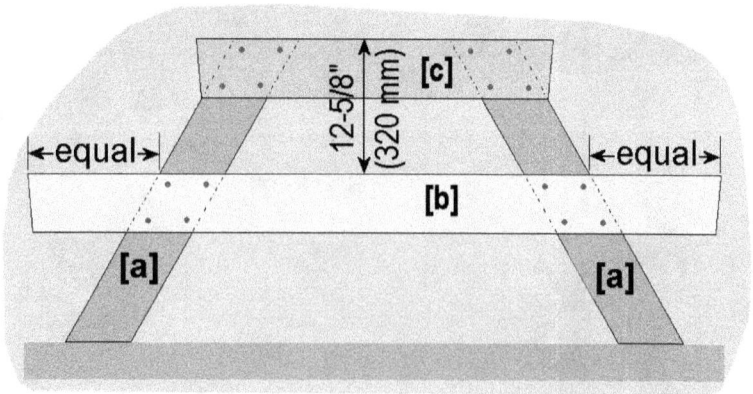

Screwing

Whenever you're fastening two pieces of wood together with screws, predrill a **clearance hole** through the top piece.

A **clearance hole** should have the same diameter or slightly larger (but not smaller) than the outside diameter of the screw threads.

This allows the screw to go through the top piece smoothly, with the threads only gripping into the bottom piece, ensuring a tight connection between the two parts.

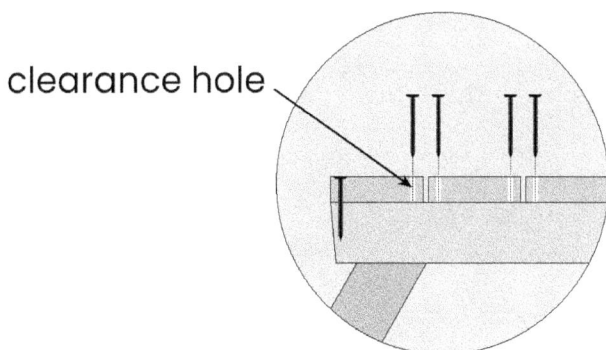

clearance hole

Step 5. Stand the frames

Clamp a block flush to the bottom of each leg, as illustrated in the drawing below. This will allow the frames to stand by themselves. Hence, you can position the frames and place the boards without needing help from another person to hold the frames upright.

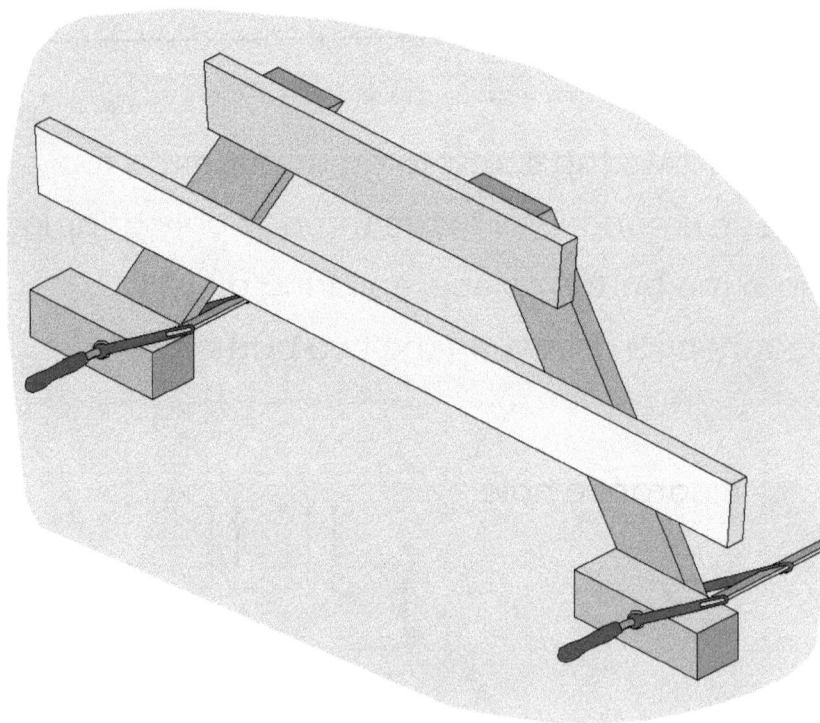

Step 6. Space the frames

Now, space the frames approximately so that when the tabletop and seat boards are positioned, they will overhang the frames at each end by 6 inches (150 mm).

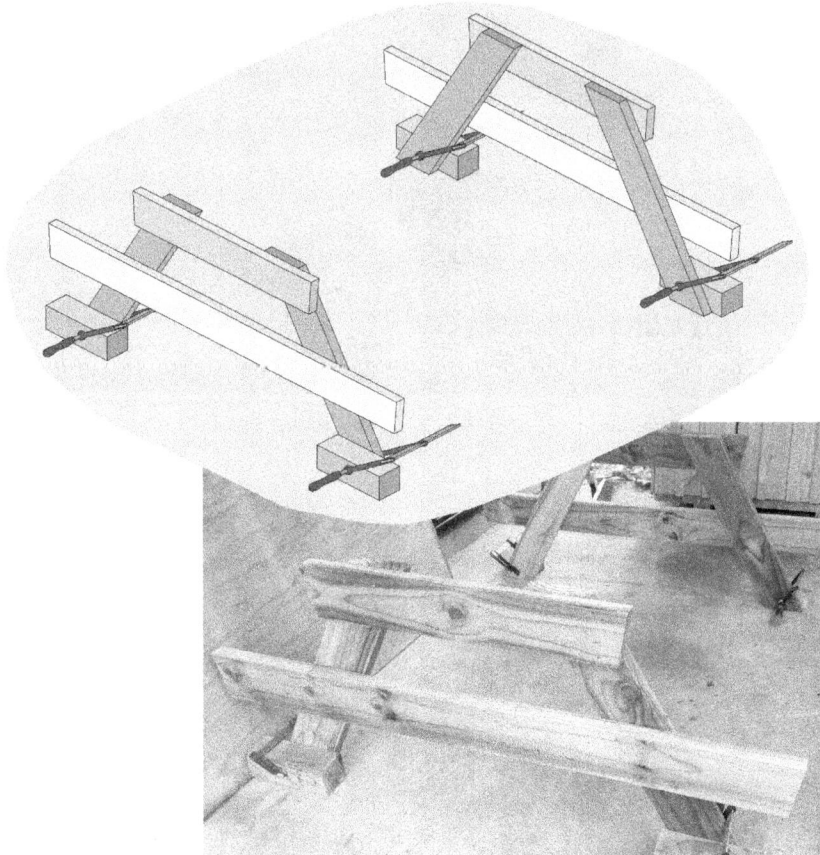

Step 7. Put on the outer boards

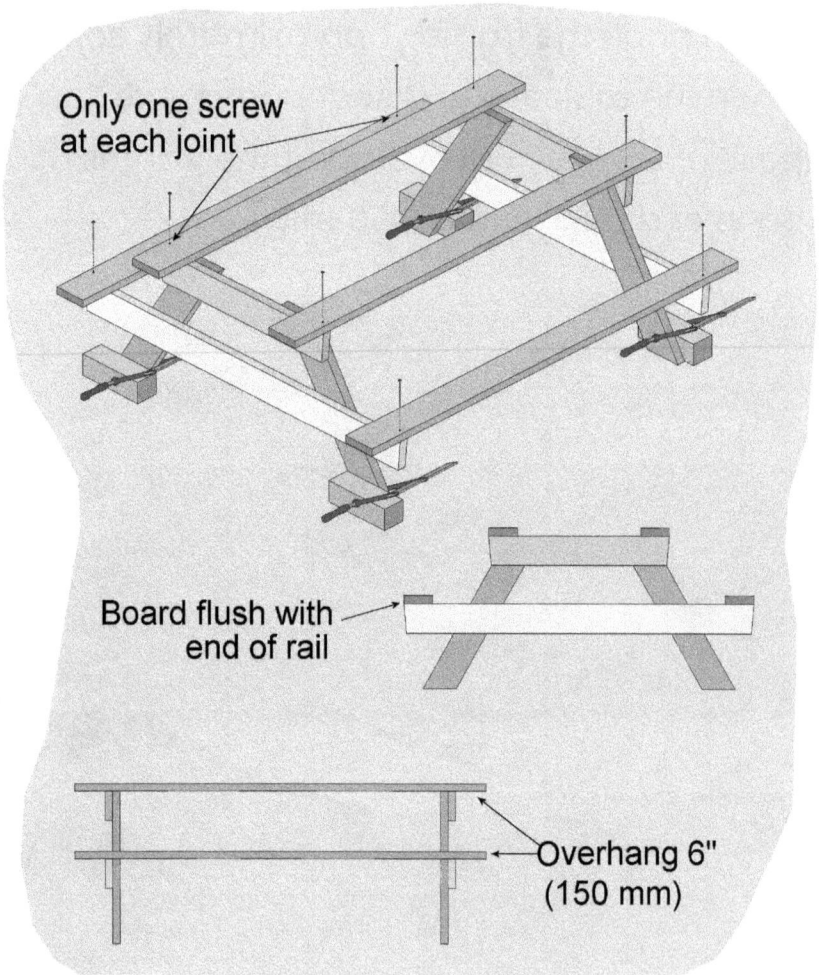

Only one screw at each joint

Board flush with end of rail

Overhang 6" (150 mm)

Put on the outer boards [explanation]

First, place the outer tabletop and seat boards onto the frame rails, having them overhang each end by 6" (150 mm). Refer to the drawing on the previous page for placement. Secure the boards with **only one screw** at each joint – for the time being. A second screw will be added when the frames have been checked square and parallel. Use 3½" (90 mm) screws positioned ¾" (19 mm) in from the edge of the board.

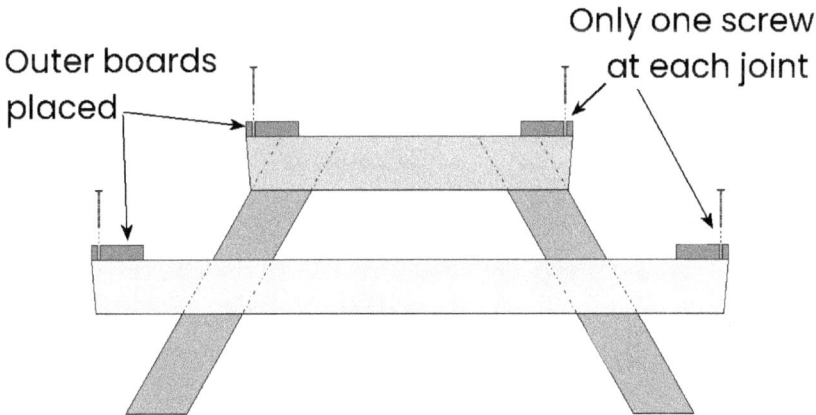

Outer boards placed

Only one screw at each joint

Is it square and parallel?

Check that the frames are square and parallel before adding a second screw at each joint.

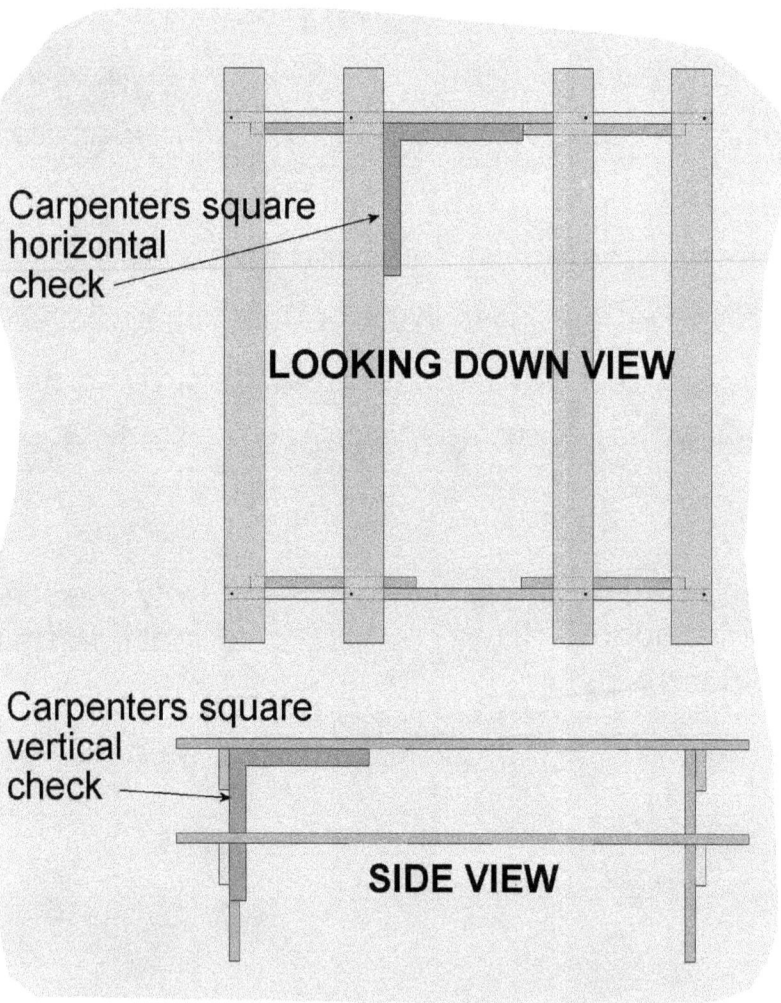

Carpenters square horizontal check

LOOKING DOWN VIEW

Carpenters square vertical check

SIDE VIEW

Is it square and parallel? [explanation]

Check that the frames are parallel, and with a carpenter's square ensure the frames are square (at right angles) to the tabletop and seat boards, both horizontally and vertically.
If necessary, make any straightening adjustments, then add a second screw to each joint.
This will hold the unit square while you continue to add the intermediate boards.

Step 8. Add the intermediate boards

Place the intermediate boards. Ensure the ends are flush and the gaps between the boards are even.

Draw a 'screw line ' across the table and seats to keep the screws in a straight line.

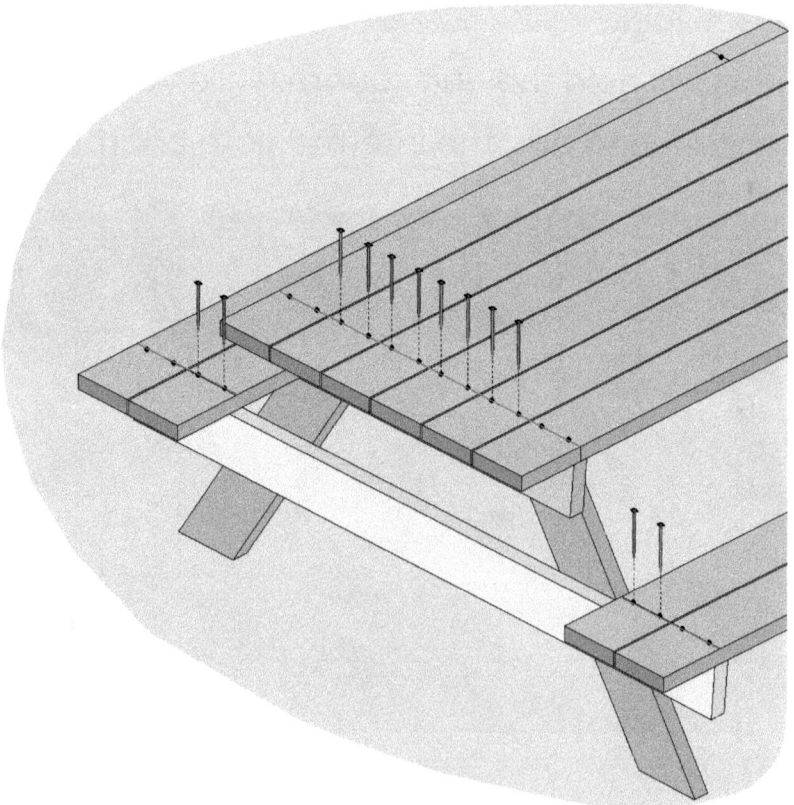

Step 9. Attach the cleats

With the table upside-down, screw cleats across the center of the seats and the tabletop.
Use two 3" (75 mm) screws positioned diagonally across each joint.

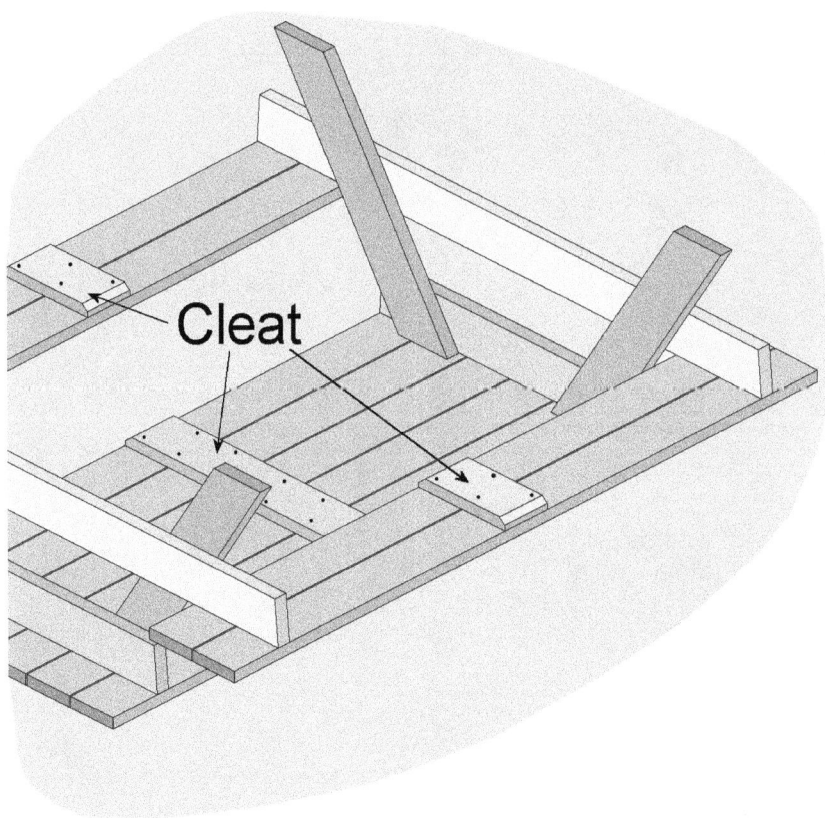

Cleat

Step 10. Add the bracing

Ensure the end-frames are square (upright) to the tabletop, and then position each brace as shown in the image below. Screw one end of the brace to the middle rail with two 3" (75 mm) screws, and the other end with 3 screws angled into the tabletop.

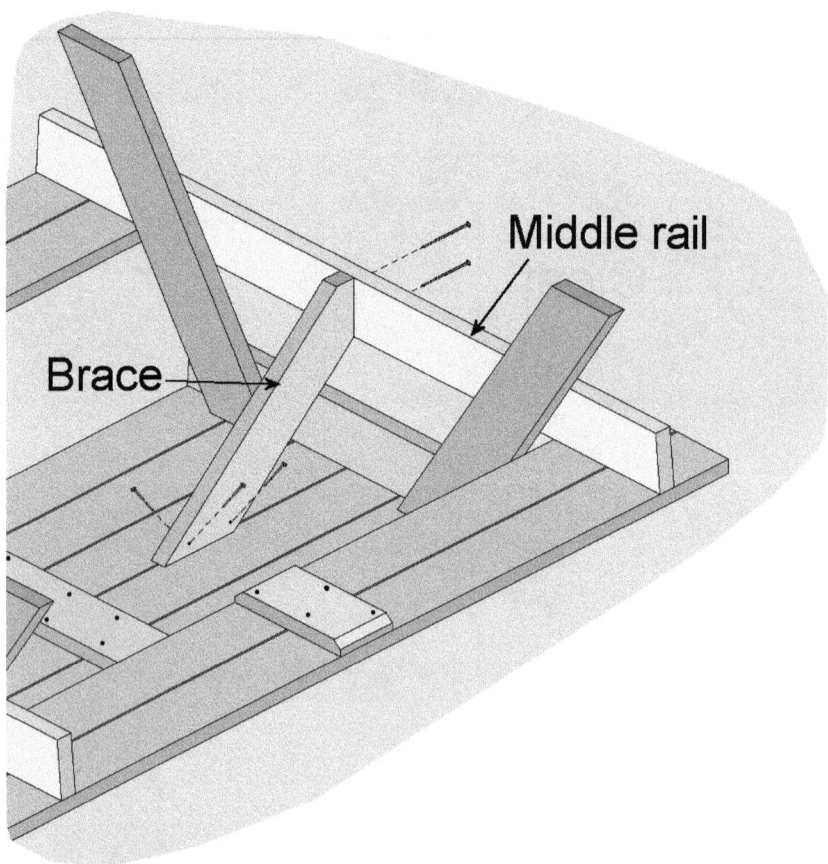

Middle rail

Brace

Step 11. Drill and bolt

Drill a bolt hole through the center of every leg and rail joint - eight altogether.
Insert 1/2" (12 mm) galvanised bolts, add washers and nuts, and tighten them up.

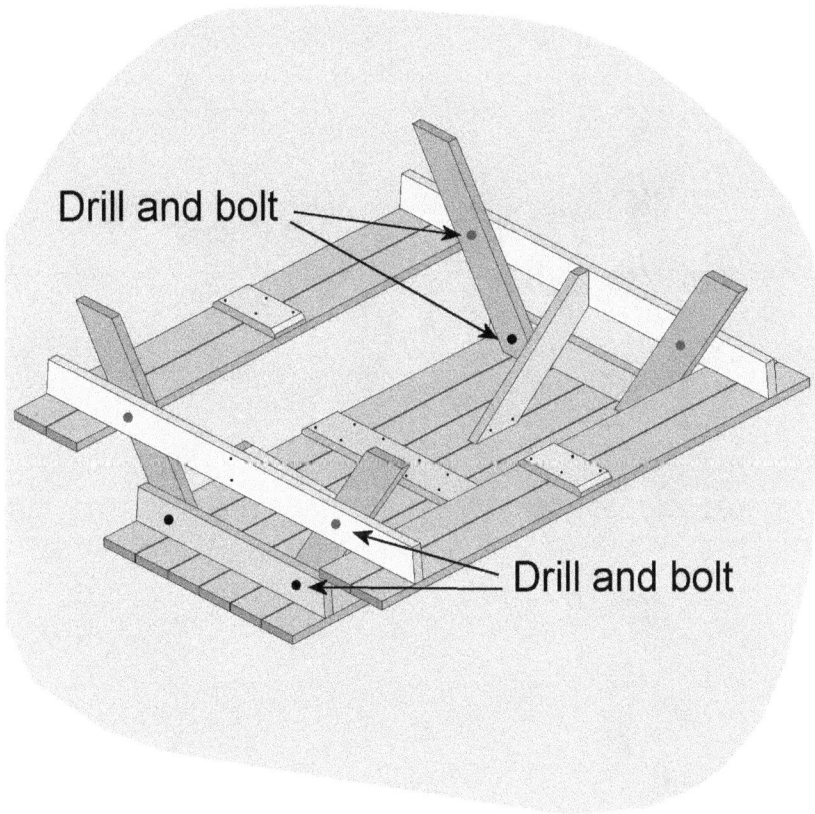

Drill and bolt

Drill and bolt

All finished!

And there it is.

A nice solid, comfortable picnic table that will seat at least six people.

The Author

Les Kenny has been creating and authoring woodworking projects for many years, with an online presence spanning almost 25 years. Although mostly retired now, he occasionally works on projects and continues to write. Les is a husband, a father of four, and a proud grandfather of seven. You can find his website at leskenny.com.

www.ingramcontent.com/pod-product-compliance
Lightning Source LLC
Chambersburg PA
CBHW071733020426
42331CB00008B/2009